Learning World
BRIDGE 4
WORKBOOK

JN122192

🌐 STEP 1	2〜5
🌐 STEP 2	6〜9
🌐 STEP 3	10〜13
🌐 STEP 4	14〜17
🌐 STEP 5	18〜21
🌐 STEP 6	22〜25
🌐 STEP 7	26〜29
🌐 STEP 8	30〜33
🌐 STEP 9	34〜37
🌐 STEP 10	38〜41
🌐 STEP 11	42〜45
🌐 STEP 12	46〜49
🌐 STEP 13	50〜53
🌐 STEP 14	54〜57
🌐 STEP 15	58〜61
🌐 STEP 16	62〜65
🌐 STEP 17	66〜69
🌐 STEP 18	70〜73

Listening Test

Pages 74-77 are Listening Tests. Audio is on the attached CD. The questions are modelled on EIKEN Test Grade 4 questions.

pp.74〜77はCDを聞きながら答えるリスニングテストです。
問題は英検4級レベルに対応しています。
音声はCD番号で頭出しができ、2回ずつくり返されます。

❶ CD 1	74
❷ CD 6	74
❸ CD 11	75
❹ CD 16	75
❺ CD 21	76
❻ CD 26	76
❼ CD 31	77
❽ CD 36	77

Let's try!
英検 4 級対応問題

❶	78
❷	79
❸	80

The "Let's try." pages are modelled on EIKEN Test Grade 4 questions.

Listening Test

pp.74〜77は英検 4 級レベルのリスニング問題です。英検対策として、付属のCDを聞いて解きましょう。

How many did you get right? 何題できたかな?

1 WORDS Dictionary **Write the words and phrases in Japanese, and then copy them in English.**

① I (　　　　　　　) _____ _____

② panda (　　　　　　　) _____ _____

③ balloon (　　　　　　　) _____ _____

④ wear (　　　　　　　) _____ _____

⑤ you (　　　　　　　) _____ _____

⑥ we (　　　　　　　) _____ _____

⑦ they (　　　　　　　) _____ _____

⑧ he (　　　　　　　) _____ _____

⑨ she (　　　　　　　) _____ _____

⑩ it (　　　　　　　) _____ _____

⑪ great (　　　　　　　) _____ _____

⑫ student (　　　　　　　) _____ _____

⑬ sleepy (　　　　　　　) _____ _____

⑭ yet (　　　　　　　) _____ _____

⑮ station (　　　　　　　) _____ _____

⑯ always (　　　　　　　) _____ _____

⑰ thirteen (　　　　　　　) _____ _____

⑱ listener (　　　　　　　) _____ _____

⑲ sport (　　　　　　　) _____ _____

⑳ punctual (　　　　　　　) _____ _____

㉑ from Japan (　　　　　　　) _____ _____

㉒ be good at (　　　　　　　) _____ _____

2 **Search the textbook for these sentences in English and write them.**

1 私はウサギです。

2 私はネコではありません。

3 私はまだ眠くありません。

4 私はここにいます。

5 私の学校は駅の前にあります。

6 私は北海道出身です。

7 私はスポーツが得意です。

8 私は時間を守ります。

3 **Choose two characters from p. 4 in the textbook and write about them.**

character

No.

character

No.

4 Fill in the blanks with **is, are** or **am**.

1 I _____ a student.

( )

5 He _____ shy.

( )

2 She _____ my sister.

( )

6 My school _____ by the station.

( )

3 We _____ friends.

( )

7 I _____ in the sixth grade.

( )

4 They _____ my classmates.

( )

5 Rewrite the above sentences using **not**.

1 _____

2 _____

3 _____

4 _____

5 _____

6 _____

7 _____

6 Rewrite the sentences into **questions**. Answer them using both **yes** and **no**.

1

Q Are you _____

A Yes, _____ No, _____

2　Q _____

　A _____

3　Q _____

　A _____

4　Q _____

　A _____

5　Q _____

　A _____

6　Q _____

　A _____

7　Q _____

　A _____

私って何者?

7 **Who I am** Write about yourself using words and phrases from the box below.

1 I am a _____

2 I am a _____

3 I am a _____

4 I am a _____

5 I am a _____

6 I am a _____

| boy | girl | daughter | son | brother | sister | friend |
| classmate | | student | grandchild | cousin | | member of... |

① WORDS Dictionary — Write the words and phrases in Japanese, and then copy them in English

① what ( ) _____ _____

② that ( ) _____ _____

③ happy ( ) _____ _____

④ angry ( ) _____ _____

⑤ this ( ) _____ _____

⑥ my ( ) _____ _____

⑦ your ( ) _____ _____

⑧ his ( ) _____ _____

⑨ stapler ( ) _____ _____

⑩ her ( ) _____ _____

⑪ our ( ) _____ _____

⑫ name ( ) _____ _____

⑬ Monday ( ) _____ _____

⑭ date ( ) _____ _____

⑮ May ( ) _____ _____

⑯ its ( ) _____ _____

⑰ their ( ) _____ _____

⑱ house ( ) _____ _____

⑲ whale ( ) _____ _____

⑳ animal ( ) _____ _____

㉑ capital city ( ) _____ _____

㉒ the earth ( ) _____ _____

㉓ unidentified flying object ( ) _____ _____

2-2

2 **Search the textbook for these sentences in English and write them.**

1 これはなあに？

2 今日は月曜日です。

3 5月7日です。

4 ［電話で］（こちらは）リサです。

5 彼の名前はポールです。

6 地球は星ではありません。

7 今日は何曜日ですか。

8 今日は何日ですか？

3 ❶ **Write the twelve months of the year.**

1月	7月
2月	8月
3月	9月
4月	10月
5月	11月
6月	12月

❷ **Write the ordinal numbers.**

1番目の	10番目の
2番目の	15番目の
3番目の	20番目の

4 **Fill in the blanks.**

1 I (私は)➡ my (私の)➡ my _____ (ぼくの消しゴム)

2 you ( )➡ _____ ( )➡ _____ (あなたのカバン)

3 he ( )➡ _____ ( )➡ _____ (彼の車)

4 she ( )➡ _____ ( )➡ _____ (彼女のかさ)

5 we ( )➡ _____ ( )➡ _____ (私たちの学校)

6 they ( )➡ _____ ( )➡ _____ (彼らの教室)

5 **Complete the sentences.**

1 This is _____ こちらは私の友達です。

2 This isn't _____ これは彼女のノートブックではありません。

3 Is this _____ これは彼のコンピューターですか？

4 That's _____ あれがあなたのカバンです。

5 These are _____ これらは私の兄のCDです。

6 Is that _____ あれはトムの本ですか？

7 That's _____ あれが私たちの教室です。

6 Write questions and answers according to the pictures.

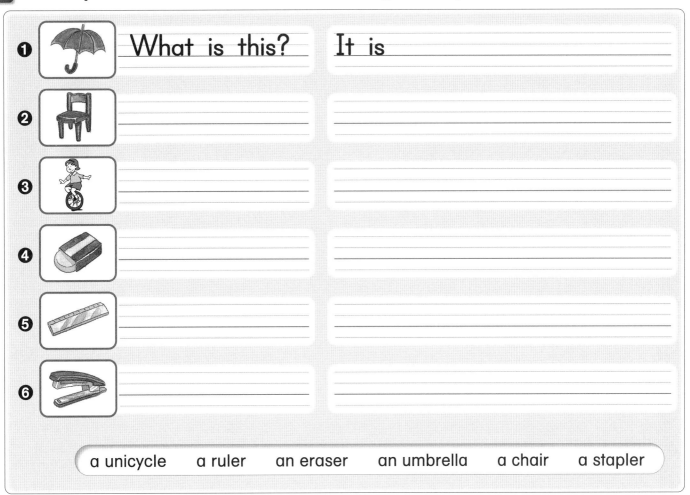

❶ What is this?   It is

❷

❸

❹

❺

❻

a unicycle   a ruler   an eraser   an umbrella   a chair   a stapler

7 Draw a line to connect the English and Japanese sentences.

English	Japanese
So what?	最近、どう？
What's up?	どうしたの？
What's wrong?	それがどうした（だから何？）
What if?	何が言いたいの？
What do you mean?	何が起こったの？
What's going on?	何が起こっているの？
What happened?	もしそうだったらどうなの？

1 WORDS   Write the phrases in Japanese, and then copy them in English.

① wash the dishes (   ) _____ _____

② give a speech (   ) _____ _____

③ set the table (   ) _____ _____

④ eat steak (   ) _____ _____

⑤ watch TV (   ) _____ _____

⑥ read the newspaper (   ) _____ _____

⑦ drive a car (   ) _____ _____

⑧ buy groceries (   ) _____ _____

⑨ feed the dog (   ) _____ _____

⑩ write a letter (   ) _____ _____

⑪ drink orange juice (   ) _____ _____

⑫ draw a map (   ) _____ _____

⑬ speak French (   ) _____ _____

⑭ study math (   ) _____ _____

3 -2

⑮ cook curry ( )

⑯ ride a bike ( )

⑰ close the door ( )

⑱ answer the phone ( )

⑲ take a picture ( )

⑳ bake a cake ( )

2 Search the textbook for these sentences in English and write them.

1 あそぼうよ。

2 ハグしないで。

3 サッカーをしてはいけません。

4 一緒に歌をうたいましょう。

5 まどをあけてくださいませんか？

6 教室では英語を話しなさい。

7 （電話が鳴っていて）
電話に出てください。

8 ピアノを練習しましょう。

3 Write the sentences in English, using the words and phrases in the box below.

① 教室の中では走ってはいけません。

② 窓をあけていただけますか？

③ （かかってきた）電話に出てください。

④ その犬にえさをあげてはいけません。

⑤ 一緒にサッカーをしようよ。

⑥ 私が行ってそれを取ってきましょうか？

⑦ ドライブに行きませんか？

⑧ 今日は外出してはいけません。

⑨ お皿をあらってください。

⑩ 今すぐ宿題をしなさい。

open the window	play soccer	feed the dog	do your homework
answer the phone		go for a drive	wash the dishes
go and get it	run	go out	

4 Write words from the box below that can go with each verb, and then write the **Japanese meaning.** * Words can be used more than once, and singular or plural is OK.

1 wash

(   )

2 read

(   )

3 open

(   )

4 answer

(   )

5 write

(   )

6 draw

(   )

7 close

(   )

the dog	the phone	the question	a letter	a story	the window	the door
a can	a box	your mouth	your hands	your hair		the shirt
your book	a map	a line	an essay	a picture		

5 私がすること
What I do Complete the sentences with action verbs from the box below.

1 I

2 I

3 I

4 I

5 I

6 I

| play | study | walk | run | cry | smile | laugh | sleep |
| talk | think | remember | breathe | climb | swim | your own ideas | |

1 WORDS Dictionary Write the words and phrases in Japanese, and then copy them in English.

① English ( )
② science ( )
③ Japanese ( )
④ music ( )
⑤ social studies ( )
⑥ arts and crafts ( )
⑦ P.E. ( )
⑧ math ( )
⑨ snake ( )
⑩ spider ( )
⑪ sister ( )
⑫ get up ( )

⑬ dictionary ( )
⑭ glasses ( )
⑮ teeth ( )
⑯ get on ( )
⑰ get off ( )
⑱ turn on ( )
⑲ turn off ( )
⑳ put on ( )
㉑ take off ( )
㉒ give up ( )
㉓ hand in ( )
㉔ run away ( )

2 Search the textbook for these sentences in English and write them.

1 お母さん、牛乳好き？

2 飲んでしまいなさい。

3 ヘビは好きですか？

4 私は犬がほしいです。

5 私は犬はほしくないです。

6 あなたは犬がほしいですか？

7 あきらめてはいけません。

8 私は1日に3回歯をみがきます。

3 Choose two characters from p.16 in the textbook and write about them.

name

① I _____ English.   ⑤ I _____ social studies.
② I _____ science.   ⑥ I _____ arts and crafts.
③ I _____ Japanese.   ⑦ I _____ P.E.
④ I _____ music.   ⑧ I _____ math.

name

① I _____ English.   ⑤ I _____ social studies.
② I _____ science.   ⑥ I _____ arts and crafts.
③ I _____ Japanese.   ⑦ I _____ P.E.
④ I _____ music.   ⑧ I _____ math.

4 Complete the sentences with appropriate verbs, and then translate the sentences into Japanese.

1 You _____ a camera in your bag. (持っている)

( )

2 You _____ my teacher's name. (知っています)

( )

3 We _____ a dictionary. (必要です)

( )

4 They _____ to school. (歩く)

( )

5 You _____ your shoes in the house. (脱ぐ)

( )

6 They _____ the train at the next station. (降りる)

( )

5 Rewrite the above sentences using **not**.

1 _____

2 _____

3 _____

4 _____

5 _____

6 _____

4-4

6 Rewrite the sentences into questions. Answer them using both yes and no.

1 Q _____

A Yes, _____ No, _____

2 Q _____

A _____ _____

3 Q _____

A _____ _____

4 Q _____

A _____ _____

5 Q _____

A _____ _____

6 Q _____

A _____ _____

7 ひまつぶしにすること
When I am free Write four things you do when you are free.

1 I _____

2 I _____

3 I _____

4 I _____

1 WORDS Write the words in Japanese, and then copy them in English and write the plural form.

① carrot ( ) <u>carrot</u>   <u>carrots</u>

② orange ( )

③ peach ( )

④ potato ( )

⑤ pig ( )

⑥ goose ( )

⑦ mouse ( )

⑧ sheep ( )

⑨ pencil ( )

⑩ desk ( )

⑪ teacher ( )

⑫ baby ( )

⑬ story ( )

⑭ dish ( )

⑮ city ( )

⑯ knife ( )

⑰ leaf ( )

⑱ life ( )

⑲ fish ( )

⑳ ruler ( )

㉑ brother ( )

㉒ bicycle ( )

㉓ class ( )

㉔ child ( )

2 Search the textbook for these sentences in English and write them.

1 それらは私の定規です。

2 硬貨を何枚持っていますか。

3 硬貨は持っていません。

4 私にかぞえさせて。

5 お金をいくらか持ってるよ。

6 あなたは子供は何人いますか?

7 私の家族では、自転車を2台持っています。

8 ラグビーには15人の選手が必要です。

3 Choose two carts from p.20 in the textbook and write about them.

cart No. I have _____ in my cart.

cart No. I have _____ in my cart.

4 Complete the sentences with appropriate words.

1 How many _____ are there?
花は何本？

2 How many _____ are there?
本は何冊？

3 How many _____ are there?
いすは何脚？

4 How many _____ do you need?
あなたは切手を何枚必要ですか。

5 How many _____ do you have in your bag?
きみはカバンの中に鉛筆を何本持っていますか？

6 How many _____ do you want?
きみは辞書が何冊ほしいですか？

5 Write sentences based on the pictures on the right.

1 This is an ant.
These are five _____

2 This is a leaf.
_____

3 That is a star.
_____

4 This is a fish.
_____

5 What is this? _____
What are these? _____

6 What is that? _____
What are those? _____

6 Translate the sentences into English.

1 私は犬が好きです。

2 私は犬を1ぴき飼っています。

3 卵をいくつ必要ですか？

4 男の兄弟は何人いますか？

5 ぼくたちは金曜日は授業が6つあります。

6 公園には4人の子供達がいます。

7 1日にどれだけ水を飲みますか？　（how much / in a day）

数について答えよう
7 About numbers Answer the questions with information about yourself.

1 How many hours do you study in a day?

2 How many countries and their capital cities do you know?

3 How many hours do you sleep in a day?

4 How many children do you want in the future?

5 Write two things which you can't see, but are in this room.

1 WORDS — Write the words in Japanese, and then copy them in English.

① where (　　　　　　) ＿＿＿＿＿＿＿ ＿＿＿＿＿＿＿

② why (　　　　　　) ＿＿＿＿＿＿＿ ＿＿＿＿＿＿＿

③ how (　　　　　　) ＿＿＿＿＿＿＿ ＿＿＿＿＿＿＿

④ when (　　　　　　) ＿＿＿＿＿＿＿ ＿＿＿＿＿＿＿

⑤ go (　　　　　　) ＿＿＿＿＿＿＿ ＿＿＿＿＿＿＿

⑥ museum (　　　　　　) ＿＿＿＿＿＿＿ ＿＿＿＿＿＿＿

⑦ bike (　　　　　　) ＿＿＿＿＿＿＿ ＿＿＿＿＿＿＿

⑧ car (　　　　　　) ＿＿＿＿＿＿＿ ＿＿＿＿＿＿＿

⑨ Saturday (　　　　　　) ＿＿＿＿＿＿＿ ＿＿＿＿＿＿＿

⑩ park (　　　　　　) ＿＿＿＿＿＿＿ ＿＿＿＿＿＿＿

⑪ Sunday (　　　　　　) ＿＿＿＿＿＿＿ ＿＿＿＿＿＿＿

⑫ sound (　　　　　　) ＿＿＿＿＿＿＿ ＿＿＿＿＿＿＿

⑬ by bus (　　　　　　) ＿＿＿＿＿＿＿ ＿＿＿＿＿＿＿

⑭ who (　　　　　　) ＿＿＿＿＿＿＿ ＿＿＿＿＿＿＿

⑮ there (　　　　　　) ＿＿＿＿＿＿＿ ＿＿＿＿＿＿＿

⑯ bag (　　　　　　) ＿＿＿＿＿＿＿ ＿＿＿＿＿＿＿

⑰ ice cream (　　　　　　) ＿＿＿＿＿＿＿ ＿＿＿＿＿＿＿

⑱ coldest (　　　　　　) ＿＿＿＿＿＿＿ ＿＿＿＿＿＿＿

⑲ many (　　　　　　) ＿＿＿＿＿＿＿ ＿＿＿＿＿＿＿

⑳ much (　　　　　　) ＿＿＿＿＿＿＿ ＿＿＿＿＿＿＿

㉑ tall (　　　　　　) ＿＿＿＿＿＿＿ ＿＿＿＿＿＿＿

㉒ often (　　　　　　) ＿＿＿＿＿＿＿ ＿＿＿＿＿＿＿

㉓ spell (　　　　　　) ＿＿＿＿＿＿＿ ＿＿＿＿＿＿＿

㉔ birthday (　　　　　　) ＿＿＿＿＿＿＿ ＿＿＿＿＿＿＿

2 Search the textbook for these sentences in English and write them.

1 ぼくはここ、木のてっぺんにいます。

2 日曜日に自転車で公園に行こうよ。

3 そこであなたは何をしたいのですか?

4 あなたは何のスポーツをしていますか?

5 きみはどんな(種類の)音楽が好き?

6 これはだれのカバンですか?

7 あなたはどのアイスクリームをほしいですか?

8 きみの誕生日はいつ?

3 Write the days of the week.

日曜日 _____

木曜日 _____

月曜日 _____

金曜日 _____

火曜日 _____

土曜日 _____

水曜日 _____

Write three places in your city.

1 _____

2 _____

3 _____

Write three kinds of transportation.

1 _____

2 _____

3 _____

4 **Write question words to complete the questions.**

① _____ are you going? —— To Tokyo.

② _____ is your English teacher? —— Mr. White is.

③ _____ bag is this? —— It's my bag.

④ _____ is my bag? —— Look! It's on the table.

⑤ _____ is your birthday? —— It's July 4th.

⑥ _____ do you like better, summer or winter? —— I like winter better.

⑦ _____ are you today? —— OK, but I have a headache.

⑧ _____ will you go to the zoo? —— On Sunday.

⑨ _____ do you use to cut paper? —— I use scissors.

⑩ _____ do you go to school? —— At seven thirty.

⑪ _____ is older, your bicycle or mine? —— Yours is older.

⑫ _____ did you go to the library? —— To read books about Japanese history.

⑬ _____ does your grandmother live? —— She lives in Los Angeles.

⑭ _____ is that tall man? —— He's my uncle.

⑮ _____ pencils are these? —— They're my pencils.

What,　Where,　When,　Who,　Why,　Which,　Whose,　What time,　How

5 Write phrases beginning with "how" to complete the questions.

① _____ does it take you to come to school? — It takes about fifteen minutes.

② _____ is your grandfather? — He's seventy years old.

③ _____ is this game? — It's three thousand two hundred yen.

④ _____ are you? — One hundred fifty-six centimeters.

⑤ _____ boys are there in this room? — There are eleven.

⑥ _____ are these books? — They're two hundred forty yen each.

⑦ _____ a short break? — That's a good idea.

⑧ _____ do you go shopping? — About once a week.

How tall, How many, How much, How old, How long, How about, How often

6 Something I did
あの日したこと
Write about something you did. Use the questions as a guide.

What did you do?   When did you do it?   Where did you do it?

Why did you do it?   How did you do it?   How did you feel?

STEP 7 -1

1 WORDS — Write the words in Japanese, and then copy them in English.

1. strange (　)
2. round (　)
3. hungry (　)
4. thirsty (　)
5. healthy (　)
6. difficult (　)
7. easy (　)
8. correct (　)
9. free (　)
10. funny (　)
11. brave (　)
12. gentle (　)
13. kind (　)
14. polite (　)
15. shy (　)
16. wise (　)
17. first (　)
18. second (　)
19. third (　)
20. expensive (　)
21. famous (　)
22. quiet (　)
23. exciting (　)
24. interesting (　)

twenty-six

㉕ boring
( )

㉖ important
( )

㉗ favorite
( )

㉘ wonderful
( )

㉙ powerful
( )

㉚ useful
( )

㉛ comfortable
( )

㉜ convenient
( )

㉝ dangerous
( )

㉞ delicious
( )

㉟ friendly
( )

㊱ necessary
( )

2 Search the textbook for these sentences in English and write them.

1 ぼくの新しい髪型どう？

2 それはかっこいい。

3 私は黒いアヒルを飼っています。

4 これは高価なカバンです。

5 なんと美しいのでしょう。

6 なんときれいな花でしょう。

7 私はなんとかわいい女の子でしょう。

8 なんと大きな犬でしょう。

3 Complete the sentences with appropriate adjectives, and then translate the sentences into Japanese.

1 I need a _____ chair. (心地よい)

(_____)

2 This is the _____ answer. (正しい)

(_____)

3 Look at the _____ sunset. (すばらしい)

(_____)

4 He is a very _____ politician. (有名な)

(_____)

5 The movie is _____. (たいくつな)

(_____)

6 My _____ color is blue. (お気に入りの)

(_____)

7 What a _____ man he is! (勇敢な)

(_____)

4 Write the sentences, putting the words in ( ) in the correct place.
(If needed, change a to an.)

1 I have a dog. (black) _____

2 These are desks. (new) _____

3 I need a box. (big) _____

4 Kyoto is a city. (old) _____

5 This is heavy. (too) _____

6 We have snow this winter. (a lot of) _____

7 I have friends at school. (many) _____

5 Translate the sentences into Japanese. (Be careful about this, these, that, and those.)

① This is my teacher Mr. Tanaka. (　　　　　　　　　　　　　)

② These are beautiful flowers. (　　　　　　　　　　　　　)

③ I want these beautiful flowers. (　　　　　　　　　　　　　)

④ Those are your shoes. (　　　　　　　　　　　　　)

⑤ Those men are police officers. (　　　　　　　　　　　　　)

⑥ Is that boy your brother? (　　　　　　　　　　　　　)

⑦ Are those your father's cars? (　　　　　　　　　　　　　)

私ってどんな人？
6 What I am like　Write about yourself using words from the box below.

1 I am _____　　5 I am _____

2 I am _____　　6 I am _____

3 I am _____　　7 I am _____

4 I am _____　　8 I am _____

strong　shy　childish　smart　optimistic　pessimistic　honest　greedy
selfish　rude　humorous　cooperative　noisy　talkative　ambitious
trustworthy　energetic　healthy　timid　brave　easygoing　creative
lazy　quiet　your own ideas

1 WORDS Dictionary Write the words and phrases in Japanese, and then copy them in English.

① reach (　　　　)

② the elderly (　　　　)

③ clean (　　　　)

④ rubble (　　　　)

⑤ carry (　　　　)

⑥ heavy (　　　　)

⑦ sign language (　　　　)

⑧ whistle (　　　　)

⑨ unicycle (　　　　)

⑩ answer (　　　　)

⑪ question (　　　　)

⑫ hamburger (　　　　)

⑬ tell (　　　　)

⑭ address (　　　　)

⑮ abacus (　　　　)

⑯ both (　　　　)

⑰ take care of (　　　　)

⑱ try it (　　　　)

⑲ made it (　　　　)

⑳ read music (　　　　)

8 -2

2 Search the textbook for these sentences in English and write them.

1 もう少しで。

2 私はお年寄りの世話をすることができます。

3 私は重いものを運ぶことができます。

4 私は手話ができます。

5 だれがその質問に答えられますか?

6 入ってもいいですか?

7 ハンバーガーを2つください。

8 お願いがあるのですが。

3 Write about things that you can do.

1 I _____ cook meals.

2 I _____ take care of _____

3 I can _____

4 I can _____

5 I can _____

6 I can _____

7 I can _____

STEP 8-3

4 Rewrite the sentences using can, and translate the new sentences into Japanese.

1 I read French.　（　　　　　　　　）

2 Ann speaks Japanese very well.　（　　　　　　　　）

3 My father plays the piano.　（　　　　　　　　）

4 Jenny reads sign language.　（　　　　　　　　）

5 Pandas climb trees.　（　　　　　　　　）

6 You get to the station by four o'clock.　（　　　　　　　　）

7 They swim in January in New Zealand.　（　　　　　　　　）

5 Rewrite the above sentences using not.

1

2

3

4

5

6

7

6 Rewrite the sentences into questions. Answer them using both **yes** and **no.**

1
Q

A Yes,   No,

2
Q

A

3
Q

A

4
Q

A

5
Q

A

6
Q

A

7
Q

A

7 できたらいいなぁ
I wish I could   Complete the sentences.

1 I wish I could

2 I wish I could

3 I wish I could

1 WORDS Dictionary Write the words and phrases in Japanese, and then copy them in English.

① pants
( )

② stripes
( )

③ natural
( )

④ dance
( )

⑤ look
( )

⑥ listen
( )

⑦ think
( )

⑧ smile
( )

⑨ run
( )

⑩ hop
( )

⑪ chat
( )

⑫ lunch
( )

⑬ tomorrow
( )

⑭ starve
( )

⑮ phone
( )

⑯ ring
( )

⑰ rain
( )

⑱ contact lenses
( )

⑲ enjoy
( )

⑳ school life
( )

㉑ have a good time
( )

㉒ leave for
( )

2 Search the textbook for these sentences in English and write them.

1 どこに行くの？

2 だれがピアノを弾いているの？

3 今、ランチを食べています。

4 お母さんは
いついらっしゃいますか？

5 今行きます。

6 おなかがすいて死にそうです。

7 電話が鳴っています。

8 明日ハワイに出発します。

3 Choose two people from p. 36 in the textbook and write about him / her.

No.

No.

4 **Rewrite the sentences using be-ing, and translate the sentences into Japanese.**

1 I read an interesting book. (　　　　　　　　　　　　　　)

2 My brother does his homework in his room. (　　　　　　　　　)

3 The telephone rings. (　　　　　　　　　　　　　　)

4 Kevin sleeps at his desk. (　　　　　　　　　　　　)

5 You listen to me carefully. (　　　　　　　　　　　)

6 Cathy waits for the bus. (　　　　　　　　　　　　)

7 My sister and I leave for Tokyo. (　　　　　　　　　)

5 **Rewrite the above sentences using not.**

1

2

3

4

5

6

7

6 Rewrite the sentences into questions. Answer them using both **yes** and **no**.

1
Q
A Yes,   No,

2
Q
A

3
Q
A

4
Q
A

5
Q
A

6
Q
A

7
Q
A

今していること
7 **What I am doing now** Complete the sentences.

1 I am _____ing now.

2 I am

3 I am

1 WORDS Write the words and phrases in Japanese, and then copy them in English.

1 hope (　　　)

2 relax (　　　)

3 pointed (　　　)

4 flat (　　　)

5 roof (　　　)

6 window (　　　)

7 chimney (　　　)

8 tail (　　　)

9 use (　　　)

10 lose (　　　)

11 choose (　　　)

12 fly (　　　)

13 wash (　　　)

14 do (　　　)

15 say (　　　)

16 this year (　　　)

17 this week (　　　)

18 swimming pool (　　　)

19 school year (　　　)

20 start (　　　)

21 come home (　　　)

22 the moon is full (　　　)

2 Search the textbook for these sentences in English and write them.

1 彼は私のことを好きですか?

2 彼は東京に住んでいるのですか?

3 彼は東京に住んでいません。

4 トムは何がほしいですか?

5 トムはいつ帰ってくるの?

6 だれがピアノを弾きますか?

7 今年の2月は29日あります。

8 日本では新学期はいつはじまりますか?

3 Fill in the blanks.

～は	～の	～を

❶ I   my   me

❷ you

～は	～の	～を

❸ he

❹ she

～は	～の	～を

❺ we

❻ they

4 Choose one house from p.40 in the textbook and write about it.

house

No.

5 **Write the sentences, changing the verb form if needed, and then translate the sentences into Japanese.**

1 My brother (study) science. _____

(_____)

2 My uncle (teach) P.E. at a high school.

(_____)

3 Lisa (finish) her homework before dinner.

(_____)

4 You and I (go) shopping today. _____

(_____)

5 Our town (have) some nice Chinese restaurants.

(_____)

6 Mr. Mahoney (use) computers in his class.

(_____)

7 Mr. and Mrs. Brown (have) three children.

(_____)

6 **Rewrite the above sentences using not.**

1 _____

2 _____

3 _____

4 _____

5 _____

Learning World BRIDGE WORKBOOK
ANSWERS pp.74～80

Let's try! ❶ ❷ ❸

p.74 Listening Test ❶ 英文とそれに関する質問文を聞いて、いちばん適切な答えを選びましょう。

| No.1 | Steve and Jenny went on a picnic last Saturday. It was sunny. They had lunch under a big tree. | Q:**Where did Steve and Jenny have lunch?** ③: Under a big tree. |

| No.2 | Susie's father likes movies. Every Saturday, he goes to the movies. He sometimes takes Susie to the movies. Susie likes musicals. | Q:**When does Susie's father go to the movies?** ①: Every Saturday. |

| No.3 | Mt. Fuji is the highest mountain in Japan. Akira and Jim climbed Mt. Fuji last week. They took a lot of photos on the top of the mountain. | Q:**What did Akira and Jim do last week?** ③: They climbed Mt. Fuji. |

| No.4 | Ben and Sally are in the sixth grade at elementary school. They both belong to the swimming club. They like swimming very much. | Q:**What grade is Ben in?** ③: The sixth grade. |

| No.5 | Kenji took his American friend, John, to Nara to see some temples. He really wanted to show John the big Buddha in Todai-ji. | Q:**Where did Kenji want to take John?** ②: To Todai-Ji. |

p.74 Listening Test ❷ 英文とそれに関する質問文を聞いて、いちばん適切な答えを選びましょう。

| No.1 | A: Hi, how are you, today? B: I'm fine. How is your mother? A: She is much better. Thank you. B: I'm glad to hear that. | Q:**How is the woman's mother?** ②: Much better. |

| No.2 | A: Hello. B: Hello. May I speak to Judy? A: Just a moment please. Who's calling? B: This is Tom speaking. | Q:**Where are they?** ②: On the phone. |

| No.3 | A: What time did you go to bed last night? B: At eleven o'clock. I got up at six this morning. A: How long did you sleep, then? B: For seven hours. | Q:**How long did she sleep?** ④: 7 hours. |

| No.4 | A: Today is my mother's birthday. B: Are you going to buy a present for her? A: Yes, I'm going to buy some flowers. B: I know a nice florist. | Q:**Where will this woman probably go next?** ①: To a florist. |

| No.5 | A: Do you know where Doctor Suzuki's clinic is? B: Suzuki? Ah, yes. Turn right at the next corner. You'll see it on your right. A: On my right? Is it a big building? B: Yes, you can't miss it. | Q:**Where is Dr. Suzuki's clinic?** ②: Right at the next corner, on the right. |

p.75 Listening Test ③ 英語の会話を聞いて、それに関する質問に答えましょう。

No.1
A: Did you do your homework today, Kenji?
B: Yes, I did.
A: Then, let's go to see the football game tonight.
B: That sounds good!

Q：**Did Kenji do his homework?**
③: Yes, he did.

No.2
A: I am thirsty. I want to have something to drink.
B: How about a glass of iced tea?
A: Well... I want to drink coffee.
B: OK. Let's drink some iced coffee.

Q：**What are they going to drink?**
①: Iced coffee.

No.3
A: Are you busy after school, Mr. Smith?
B: No, I'm not. What's up?
A: I'd really like some help with my homework.
B: OK. Come to my room at three thirty.

Q：**What time are they meeting?**
④: At three thirty.

No.4
A: Let's go swimming tomorrow afternoon.
B: OK. But it will be rainy tomorrow.
A: I don't mind, do you?
B: No. So let's go!

Q：**How will the weather be tomorrow afternoon?**
③: It will be rainy.

No.5
A: Where did you go for your vacation, Greg?
B: I went to Sendai. We had great weather.
A: Really? How did you go there?
B: We flew from Kansai airport.

Q：**How did Greg get to Sendai?**
①: By plane.

p.75 Listening Test ④ 英文とそれに関する質問文を聞いて、いちばん適切な答えを選びましょう。

No.1
Ben usually walks to school, but yesterday it was raining very hard.
So his mother drove him to school.

Q：**How did Ben go to school yesterday?**
③: By car.

No.2
Andrew wants to be a musician. He has piano lessons on
Saturday and he practices hard every day. He can also play the violin.

Q：**When does Andrew have piano lessons?**
①: On Saturday.

No.3
Last summer holidays, Yukako and her family went to Okinawa.
She really enjoyed the nice sunny weather, and
she and her family went swimming every day.

Q：**How was the weather in Okinawa?**
③: Sunny.

No.4
Susie is good at math, but her friend, Sally, isn't.
She often helps Sally with her homework.
In return, Sally helps Susie with her science reports.

Q：**What subject is Susie good at?**
②: Math.

No.5
Kazuko wanted to make an apple pie, but there were no apples.
She went to the supermarket to by some and she met her aunt there.

Q：**What did Kazuko buy at the supermarket?**
①: Some apples.

p.76 Listening Test ⑤ 英文とそれに関する質問文を聞いて、いちばん適切な答えを選びましょう。

No.1
A: Brad, are you busy tonight?
B: No, not really. Why?
A: We're going to the movies tonight.
  Would you like to come?
B: Sure.

Q：**Will Brad go to the movies tonight?**
④: Yes.

No.2
A: Cindy, how's everything?
B: Great. And how are you?
A: Well, I think I have a cold.
B: That's too bad.

Q：**What's wrong?**
④: Cindy's friend has a cold.

No.3
A: Mr. Tanaka is going back to Japan.
B: Really? When?
A: Next month. Let's buy him a present.
B Yes, let's.

Q：**Why will they buy a present?**
③: Mr. Tanaka is going back to Japan.

No.4
A: Emi! What are you doing here?
B: Happy birthday! This is for you.
A: Wow, thanks a lot.
B: I hope you like it.

Q：**Which is true?**
②: Emi has a present for her friend.

No.5
A: Hello.
B: Hello. This is Martin. May I speak to Cathy, please?
A: Cathy? Cathy doesn't live here. You have the wrong number.
B: Oh, I'm sorry.

Q：**Why is Martin sorry?**
④: Martin has the wrong number.

No.1
A: Did you go to the soccer game last Sunday, Lisa?
B: No, it was raining. I watched it on TV.
A: Oh, I see. Which team won?
B: I don't know. I fell asleep.

Q: Did Lisa go to the soccer game last Sunday?
④: No, she didn't.

No.2
A: Do you like hiking, Pam?
B: Yes, I do. I often go with my brother.
 Do you want to come with us some time, Mark?
A: I'd love to. Do you know any good places?
B: Yes, I know many good places around here.

Q: Does Mark want to go hiking with Pam?
①: Yes, he does.

No.3
A: Mom, where are you?
B: I'm here in the living room, Andy.
 Can you come and help me move the TV?
A: Just a minute. I'm coming!
B: That's OK. Your father is here. He'll help me.

Q: Who will help Mom move the TV?
②: Andy's father will.

No.4
A: Dad, what are we having for dinner tonight?
B: Steak and vegetables. Why?
A: I really want to go to the pizza place.
B: The pizza place? OK. We can go on Friday, but tonight we'll eat at home.
A: Thanks, Dad.

Q: Will they eat pizza tonight?
③: No, they won't.

No.5
A: Are you cold, Lucy?
B: No, but if you're cold, shall I close the window?
A: No, that's OK. I'll get a sweater.
B: Here, this is yours.

Q: Did Lucy close the window?
①: No, she didn't.

No.1
Steve went shopping this morning, because he wanted to buy a present for his girlfriend. He bougnt her a CD and he will give it to her tonight.

Q: When did Steve go shopping?
②: This morning.

No.2
Karl is an exchange student from Germany.
He has been in Japan for three months and he really enjoys his life here.
He has made many friends.

Q: How long has Karl been in Japan?
①: For three months.

No.3
Today Takeshi was late for school.
Last night there was a lot of snow and all the trains were late this morning.
Takeshi was twenty minutes late for school, but so was his teacher!

Q: Why was Takeshi late for school?
④: Because the trains were late.

No.4
Jenny was angry with her friend, Chris, today.
He forgot it was her birthday and didn't say "Happy Birthday" to her.

Q: What was special about today?
③: It was Jenny's birthday.

No.5
On the way to school today, Hironori found some money on the street.
It was a lot of money and Hironori wanted to buy some new sneakers.
But he took the money to the police station.

Q: What did Hironori do with the money?
③: He took the money to the police.

No.1
A: Hello. May I help you?
B: Yes, I'm looking for a blue shirt.
A: How about this one? It's a very popular item.
B: It's nice, but I'm looking for a dark blue shirt.

Q: Will the man buy the shirt?
④: No, he won't buy it.

No.2
A: Thank you for letting me stay at your house, John.
B: No. It was my pleasure. I hope you had a good time, Sue.
A: Yes I did. You were so kind to me.
B: Why don't you come again during the summer vacation?

Q: Did Sue enjoy her stay?
②: Yes, she did.

No.3
A: Do you know what time the Banana Cafe closes?
B: Hm, I think it's open until 9:15 tonight.
A: Would you like to go there with me?
B: I'm sorry, I have to look after my little brother this evening.
 How about tomorrow?

Q: What time does the cafe close?
④: It closes at 9:15.

No.4
A: Hello. Is Cathy there?
B: I'm sorry. She is out now. May I take a message?
A: Please tell her Sam called and that tomorrow's party starts at 6 o'clock.
B: At 6 tomorrow. I'll give her the message when she gets back.

Q: Why did Sam call Cathy?
③: To tell Cathy about the party.

No.5
A: Are you going shopping tomorrow?
B: I'll go if it is fine tomorrow.
A: What will you do if it rains?
B: I'll stay home and do my homework.

Q: What will she do if it doesn't rain tomorrow?
①: She will go shopping.

Let's try. 1 p.78

■日本文の意味を表すように、①～⑤までならべかえましょう。

❶ 学校からの帰り道にケンに会いました。 I met (①Ken ②on ③home ④way ⑤my) from school.

I met ____ Ken on my way home ____ from school.

❷ これが私の町でいちばん高い建物です。 This is (①building ②tallest ③in ④the ⑤my) town.

This is ____ the tallest building in my ____ town.

❸ 放課後に野球をしてもいいですよ。 You (①play ②baseball ③after ④may ⑤school).

You ____ may play baseball after school ____.

❹ 私は今日初めてマリ子に会いました。 I met (①for ②first ③Mariko ④the ⑤time) today.

I met ____ Mariko for the first time ____ today.

❺ どれくらい京都に滞在するつもりですか？ How long (①you ②going ③stay ④are ⑤to) in Kyoto?

How long ____ are you going to stay ____ in Kyoto?

❻ 私は、ユキをお誕生日パーティーに招待するつもりです。 I will (①Yuki ②to ③invite ④birthday ⑤my) party.

I will ____ invite Yuki to my birthday ____ party.

❼ 今年の夏休みは、何をするつもりですか？

What are (①you ②going ③do ④to ⑤during) this summer vacation?

What are you going to do during   this summer vacation?

❽ 私は母よりずっと背が高いです。 I am (①taller ②much ③than ④mother ⑤my).

I am ____ much taller than my mother ____.

❾ 遅れてすみませんでした。 I (①sorry ②late ③am ④I ⑤am).

I ____ am sory I am late ____.

❿ 私は何か冷たい飲みものがほしい。 I (①something ②drink ③to ④cold ⑤want).

I ____ want something cold to drink ____.

⓫ 祖母はめがねをさがしています。 Grandmother (①for ②looking ③is ④her ⑤glasses).

Grandmother ____ is looking for her glasses ____

Let's try. 2 p.79

■( )の中に最も適当なことばを選びましょう。

❶ Will you (__pass__) me the sugar, please?
　①some ②pass ③do ④like

❷ You have to take (__off__) your shoes when you enter the house.
　①on ②in ③off ④of

❸ (__Don't__) smoke. You are eighteen years old.
　①Isn't ②Not ③Don't ④Aren't

❹ I like summer. (__How__) about you?
　①How ②How many ③Where ④Who

❺ Mt. Fuji is 3776 meters (__high__).
　①long ②taller ③high ④times

❻ My apartment is (__on__) the second floor.
　①on ②in ③at ④for

❼ Thank you very much (__for__) the nice present.
　①in ②but ③for ④did

❽ What (__were__) you doing at nine o'clock last night?
　①are ②were ③is ④am

❾ A: How much is this shirt?
　B: (__870 yen.__)
　①870 yen. ②45 minutes. ③Thank you. ④OK.

❿ A: Here's a present for you.　B: Thank you.
　A: (__You're welcome.__)
　①OK. ②Of course. ③You're welcome. ④I am sorry.

⓫ A: Can you speak English?
　B: (__Just a little.__)
　①I like it very much. ②Just a little. ③Thank you. ④Yes, I do.

⓬ A: I feel much better today.
　B: (__I am glad to hear that.__)
　①That's too bad. ②Thank you. ③I am sorry. ④I am glad to hear that.

Let's try. 3 p.80

■( )の中に最も適当なことばを選びましょう。

❶ A: Shall we go out to have dinner tonight?
　B: (No, let's not.). I want to stay at home and watch TV.
　①Yes, please. ②No, let's not. ③You're welcome. ④OK.

❷ A: Show me your photo. Who took it?
　B: (My father did.)
　①I like it. ②My father did. ③That's my dog. ④This is a camera.

❸ A: (I beg your pardon?)
　I could not understand what you said.
　①Yes, please. ②I beg your pardon? ③Of course. ④I did.

❹ A: How about a cup of coffee?
　B: (No, thank you.). I am not thirsty.
　①Sugar, please. ②I like coffee. ③I like tea. ④No, thank you.

❺ A: (May I help you?)
　B: Yes, I am looking for a sweater for my mother.
　①May I help you? ②Where is my mother? ③What is it? ④How much is it?

❻ A: This book is not mine. Whose book is this?
　B: (It's hers.)
　①This is a book. ②It's hers. ③I like this book. ④No, thank you.

❼ A: What did Ken give you last night?
　B: (He gave me a nice bag.)
　① He gave you a nice bag. ② I gave him a nice bag. ③ He gave me a nice bag. ④ You gave me a nice bag.

❽ A: What month comes after June?
　B: (July dose.)
　①July does. ②March does. ③August does. ④July is.

❾ A: Shall I open the window?
　B: (Yes, please.)
　①Yes, let's. ②Yes, please. ③You're welcome. ④That's all.

❿ A: What time did you eat lunch, today?
　B: (At noon.)
　①At lunch. ②A hot dog. ③In the living room. ④At noon.

⓫ Why are you late (for) school?
　①on ②in ③for ④under

⓬ Be kind (to) old people.
　①for ②to ③on ④with

⓭ (September) is the ninth month of the year.
　①February ②November ③September ④October

⑥ _____

⑦ _____

7 Rewrite the sentences into questions.

1 _____
_____

2 _____
_____

3 _____
_____

4 _____
_____

5 _____
_____

6 _____
_____

7 _____
_____

8 Complete the sentences with the appropriate pronouns.

① 私は彼をよく知っています。

I know _____ very well.

② 彼女を招待しましょうよ。

Let's invite _____ .

③ (私を) 押さないで！

Don't push _____ !

④ 後で折り返しあなたにお電話します。

I'll call _____ back later.

⑤ 彼らをここに連れてきてください。

Please bring _____ here.

9 自分と他の人で違うこと
He does, but I don't   Choose someone (a friend or family member), and complete the sentences.

My _____ has _____ , but I don't _____.

My _____ likes _____ , but I don't_____.

1 WORDS Dictionary **Write the words and phrases in Japanese, and then copy them in English.**

① annoying (　　　　　)

② around (　　　　　)

③ under (　　　　　)

④ bench (　　　　　)

⑤ lake (　　　　　)

⑥ behind (　　　　　)

⑦ over (　　　　　)

⑧ mountain (　　　　　)

⑨ cottage (　　　　　)

⑩ at night (　　　　　)

⑪ in the morning (　　　　　)

⑫ on Sunday (　　　　　)

⑬ on July twentieth (　　　　　)

⑭ in April (　　　　　)

⑮ in 2020 (　　　　　)

⑯ for six hours (　　　　　)

⑰ before ten (　　　　　)

⑱ after ten (　　　　　)

⑲ by bike (　　　　　)

⑳ by ten thirty (　　　　　)

㉑ until ten thirty (　　　　　)

㉒ in English (　　　　　)

㉓ usually (　　　　　)

㉔ between A and B (　　　　　)

2 Search the textbook for these sentences in English and write them.

1 屋根の上に2人の子供達がいますか？

2 バスは新宿行きです。

3 私は英語で日記をつけています。

4 木の下に1ぴきのキツネがいます。

5 私は午後9時半までテレビでニュースを見ます。

6 私はたいてい8時間寝ます。

7 あなたの町には大きな公園はありますか？

8 1日は24時間あります。

3 Fill in the blanks and complete the sentences.

1 I get up _____ six o'clock _____ the morning.

2 I go to school _____ bus _____ my sister.

3 The bus is bound _____ Shinjuku. I get off the bus _____ Midorigaoka.

4 My school is _____ City Hall.

5 _____ night, I keep a diary _____ English.

6 I usually take a bath _____ eight and nine.

7 I watch the news on TV _____ 9:30 pm.

8 I go to bed _____ ten o'clock. I usually sleep _____ eight hours.

| around | in | for | at | by | until | in front of | at | between | with |

4 Complete the sentences with the correct prepositions.

1 I go to bed —————— ten o'clock. (10時に)

2 I always go to school —————— bus. (バスで)

3 Your cap is —————— the sofa. (ソファの下に)

4 This airplane is —————— London. (ロンドン行き)

5 Look —————— me. (私を見る)

6 Listen —————— me. (私の言うことに耳を傾ける)

7 He watches the news on TV —————— nine thirty. (9時30分まで)

8 He goes to bed —————— eleven o'clock. (11 時までに)

5 Translate the sentences into Japanese, and rewrite them using **not**.

1 There is a department store in front of the station. ( )

2 There are four seasons in a year. ( )

3 There is a tall building behind the hospital. ( )

4 There are many animals in this zoo. ( )

5 There is a good shopping center in this town. ( )

6 **Rewrite the sentences into questions. Answer them using both yes and no.**

1
Q _____
A Yes, _____ No, _____

2
Q _____
A _____

3
Q _____
A _____

4
Q _____
A _____

5
Q _____
A _____

7 **Write the sentences, putting the words in order.**

1 私は日曜日は11時より後に寝ます。   (eleven / on / go to bed / Sunday / after / o'clock / I).

_____

2 私はたいてい8時から10時の間にお風呂に入ります。   (a bath / usually / between / eight and ten / take / I).

_____

8 私のいる場所
Around me   Complete the sentences.

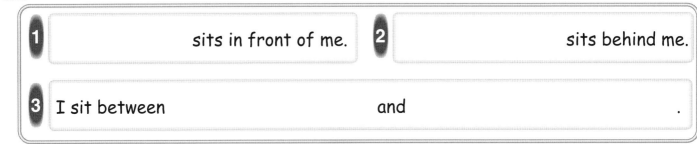

1 _____ sits in front of me.   2 _____ sits behind me.

3 I sit between _____ and _____ .

1 WORDS Dictionary Write the words and phrases in Japanese, and then copy them in English.

① slowly ( )

② tight ( )

③ early ( )

④ easily ( )

⑤ loudly ( )

⑥ every day ( )

⑦ late ( )

⑧ fast ( )

⑨ regularly ( )

⑩ happily ( )

⑪ well ( )

⑫ hard ( )

⑬ carefully ( )

⑭ soon ( )

⑮ ago ( )

⑯ here ( )

⑰ upstairs ( )

⑱ never ( )

⑲ sometimes ( )

⑳ quietly ( )

㉑ gently ( )

㉒ clearly ( )

㉓ poorly ( )

㉔ neatly ( )

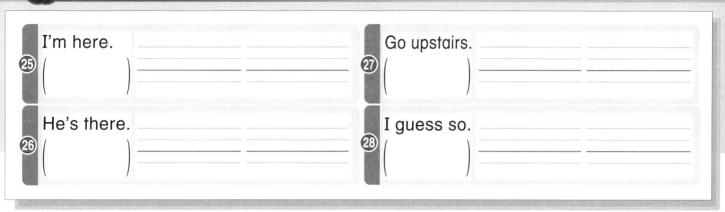

㉕ I'm here. (　　　　　)

㉖ He's there. (　　　　　)

㉗ Go upstairs. (　　　　　)

㉘ I guess so. (　　　　　)

2 Search the textbook for these sentences in English and write them.

1 しっかりつかまっていなさい。

2 あなたは英語を上手に話しますね。

3 その箱を慎重にあけてください。

4 あなたはいつも親切ですね。

5 私はその男性に2日前に会ったよ。

6 私はポップミュージックが大好きです。

7 あなたはいつも私に怒ってる。

8 私は外国に行きたい。

3 Draw a line to connect the English and Japanese sentences.

1 I guess so. •　　　　　• ここ最高!

2 Have a good time. •　　　　　• 同感!

3 I don't care. •　　　　　• 楽しんでね。

4 I agree. •　　　　　• たぶんそうだと思う。

5 I like it here. •　　　　　• 気にしない。

4 Write the sentences with appropriate words, and then translate the sentences into Japanese.

1 Mark speaks Japanese (上手に) . ( )

_____
_____

2 My grandmother speaks (はっきりと) . ( )

_____
_____

3 She is (いつも) smiling (しあわせそうに) . ( )

_____
_____

4 Cheetahs can run (とても) (速く) . ( )

_____
_____

5 I (決して～しない) forget my homework. ( )

_____
_____

6 This shirt is (～すぎる) small for me. ( )

_____
_____

7 You drive (～すぎる) (速く) . Drive (もっと) (ゆっくりと) . ( )

_____
_____

5 Write the sentences, putting the words in ( ) in the correct place.

1 Ann is very busy on Saturday. (often)

_____
_____

2 Daisuke goes to school by train. (always)

_____
_____

3 Eve's mother comes home early on Wednesday. (sometimes)

_____
_____

4 I am late for school. (never)

_____
_____

6 **Write the sentences in English.**

1 私はここが好き！── 私もよ。

2 もっと注意深く聞きなさい。

3 息を深く吸って！

4 私は朝早く起きます。

5 私はサッカーがあまり上手ではありません。

6 ぼくは自転車を持っていません。── ぼくも持っていません。

7 私は和食があまり好きではありません。

7 私は…
How I do things Write about yourself using words from the box below.

1 I run _____

2 I speak _____

3 I sing _____

4 I am _____ friendly.

5 I am _____ kind to everyone.

| fast | slowly | clearly | softly | loudly | quietly | much | well | poorly |
| always | sometimes | never | often | your own ideas |

1 WORDS Dictionary Write the words and phrases in Japanese, and then copy them in English.

1 read aloud ( )

2 many times ( )

3 memorize ( )

4 sentence ( )

5 movie ( )

6 listen to ( )

7 beach ( )

8 outside ( )

9 astronaut ( )

10 scientist ( )

11 call back ( )

12 this evening ( )

13 program ( )

14 weekend ( )

15 do my best ( )

16 make friends ( )

17 take a walk ( )

18 catch up ( )

19 be late for ( )

2 Search the textbook for these sentences in English and write them.

1 最善をつくします。

2 私はアメリカ出身の友達を作ります。

3 彼は宇宙飛行士になるでしょう。

4 彼女はすぐに追いつくでしょう。

5 私たちは来年13歳になります。

6 明日は雨は降らないでしょう。

7 手伝ってくれますか？
もちろん。

8 私は5時までに帰ります。

3 Choose 3 characters from p.52 in the textbook and write what they'll do to be good English speakers.

name

name

name

4 Write the sentences using will, and then translate the sentences into Japanese.

1 I meet you soon. (   )
_____
_____
_____

2 There is a big hotel in front of the station. (   )
_____
_____
_____

3 I am home in ten minutes. (   )
_____
_____
_____

4 I get a taxi. (   )
_____
_____
_____

5 It is warmer tomorrow. (   )
_____
_____
_____

5 Rewrite the above sentences using not.

1 _____
_____

2 _____
_____

3 _____
_____

4 _____
_____

5 _____
_____

6 Rewrite the sentences into questions. Answer them using both yes and no.

1 **Q** _____
_____

A Yes, _____   No, _____
_____

2 **Q** _____
_____

A _____
_____

3

Q _____

A _____

4

Q _____

A _____

5

Q _____

A _____

7 Complete and write the sentences using **be going to.**

① お昼に何を食べる？　_____ for lunch?

② 今日は何をするつもり？　_____

③ Lisaは私の家に泊まりに来ます。_____ come and stay with us.

④ 楽しくなるね。　It _____ a lot of fun.

⑤ 私はプレゼントを買います。　I _____ buy a present.

8 将来の成功のために
For my successful future   Complete the sentences.

1 I will _____

2 I will _____

3 I will _____

4 I will _____

1 WORDS

Write the words in Japanese, and then write the comparatives and superlatives in English.

① tall
(   )   taller   tallest   _____

② big
(   )   _____   _____

③ cheap
(   )   _____   _____

④ nice
(   )   _____   _____

⑤ happy
(   )   _____   _____

⑥ easy
(   )   _____   _____

⑦ large
(   )   _____   _____

⑧ pretty
(   )   _____   _____

⑨ good
(   )   _____   _____

⑩ interesting
(   )   _____   _____

⑪ difficult
(   )   _____   _____

⑫ famous
(   )   _____   _____

popular
⑬ (   )

strong
⑭ (   )

young
⑮ (   )

2 Search the textbook for these sentences in English and write them.

1 世界で一番美しい女性はだれだ？

2 私は良い方を取ります。

3 ぼくは3びきの中で一番年下です。

4 ぼくは家族の中で一番年下です。

5 ぼくの家は3つの中で一番頑丈です。
かんじょう
（強いです）

6 AとBではどちらが重いですか？

7 ぼくはきみより上手にピアノを弾きます。

8 1インチは1センチより長い。

3 Choose one family from p. 56 in the textbook and write about how tall they are.

name

4 Complete the sentences using the comparative form of the words in (   ).

① I am ___taller than___ my mother.　(tall)

② May is _____ March.　(warm)

③ This question is _____ that one.　(easy)

④ Your dog is _____ my dog.　(pretty)

⑤ The moon is _____ the earth.　(small)

⑥ My bag is _____ your bag.　(old)

5 ～よりも～です Write the sentences, putting the words in order.

① 私は、Mike より若い。 (I / younger / am / than / Mike).

② 3年前、私はお母さんよりずっと背が低かった。
(I / shorter / was / much / my / mother / three years ago / than).

③ この辞書は、あの辞書よりぶ厚いのに、あの辞書よりずっと安い。
(This dictionary / thicker / that dictionary / is / than),
but (this dictionary / cheaper / that dictionary / is / much / than).

but

④ 私はもっと良いものがほしいです。 (want / the better / I / to / get / one).

⑤ 白雪姫はあなたよりもっと美しい。 (is / you / Snow White / beautiful / than / more).

6 一番〜です Write the sentences, putting the words in order.

① 東京は日本で一番大きな都市です。   (Tokyo / biggest / is / in / Japan / city / the).

② 日本では秋が1年で一番カラフルな季節です。   (Fall / season / is / in / the / most colorful / Japan).

③ このクラスでだれが一番走るのが速いですか？   (Who / the / fastest / in / this class / runner / is).

④ ナイル川は世界で一番長い川です。   (The Nile / the longest / of all the rivers / is / in the world).

7 Draw a line to connect the English and Japanese sentences.

❶ The sooner, the better. •   • ずいぶん気分が良くなりました。

❷ I feel much better. •   • 全力を尽くします。

❸ First come, first served. •   • ぼくはもう子供じゃありません。

❹ I'll do my best. •   • 先着順。

❺ I am no longer a child. •   • 早ければ早いほど良い。

8 Myself and others   いろいろな見方   Complete the sentences.

❶ I am taller than _____ but I am shorter than _____.

❷ I am younger than _____ but I am older than _____.

❸ I am stronger than _____ but I am weaker than _____.

❹ I am bigger than _____ but I am smaller than _____.

1 WORDS Dictionary **Write the words and phrases in Japanese, and then copy them in English.**

① still (　　　　　)

② shopping mall (　　　　　)

③ food court (　　　　　)

④ kitchen (　　　　　)

⑤ bacon and eggs (　　　　　)

⑥ breakfast (　　　　　)

⑦ busy (　　　　　)

⑧ tired (　　　　　)

⑨ exam (　　　　　)

⑩ yesterday (　　　　　)

⑪ sick (　　　　　)

⑫ absent (　　　　　)

⑬ last week (　　　　　)

⑭ last night (　　　　　)

⑮ taking a shower (　　　　　)

⑯ working in the garden (　　　　　)

⑰ on the phone (　　　　　)

⑱ all day long (　　　　　)

⑲ at that time (　　　　　)

2 Search the textbook for these sentences in English and write them.

1 JJはフードコートで友達と食べていました。

2 Eveは友達と電話でおしゃべりをしていました。

3 Jasonは1日中そうじをしていました。

4 いったいどうしたの?

5 先週はだれが休んでいましたか?

6 私は先週病気で寝ていました。

7 今日の朝ご飯はとてもおいしかったです。

8 あなたは昨晩の8時にどこにいましたか?

3 Choose items from p.60 in the textbook and write about what he / she was doing.

1 at 8 o'clock in the morning

(JJ/ Eve) was

2 at 10:30 in the morning

3 at 3 o'clock in the afternoon

4 at 10 o'clock at night

4 Complete the sentences using the correct form of the be verb, and then translate them into Japanese.

1 It _____ Sunday today.
(   )

2 It _____ Saturday yesterday.
(   )

3 It _____ Monday tomorrow.
(   )

4 I _____ at Tokyo Station now.
(   )

5 I _____ at a restaurant in Shinjuku two hours ago.
(   )

6 I _____ eating lunch with my friends then.
(   )

7 I _____ in Nagoya in two hours.
(   )

8 Tom and his father _____ playing badminton now.
(   )

9 They _____ playing it when I came home one hour ago.
(   )

10 They _____ going to play in a badminton tournament next Sunday.
(   )

5 Rewrite the above sentences using not.

1

2

3

4

5

6

7

⑧ _____

⑨ _____

⑩ _____

6 Rewrite the sentences into questions.

1 _____

2 _____

3 _____

4 _____

5 _____

6 _____

7 _____

8 _____

9 _____

10 _____

7 私の過去、現在、未来
My past, present, and future Complete the sentences.

1 I was _____ when I was _____ years old.

2 I am _____ now.

3 I will be _____ when I am twenty-four years old.

1 WORDS *Dictionary* **Write the words and phrases in Japanese, and then copy them in English and write the past tense.**

① play ( ) *play   played*

② make ( )

③ watch ( )

④ study ( )

⑤ buy ( )

⑥ do ( )

⑦ take a bath ( )

⑧ eat ( )

⑨ wash ( )

⑩ want ( )

⑪ start ( )

⑫ stop ( )

⑬ run ( )

⑭ come ( )

⑮ see ( )

⑯ go ( )

⑰ speak ( )

⑱ write ( )

⑲ drink ( )

⑳ choose ( )

㉑ have ( )

㉒ meet ( )

㉓ sit ( )

㉔ find ( )

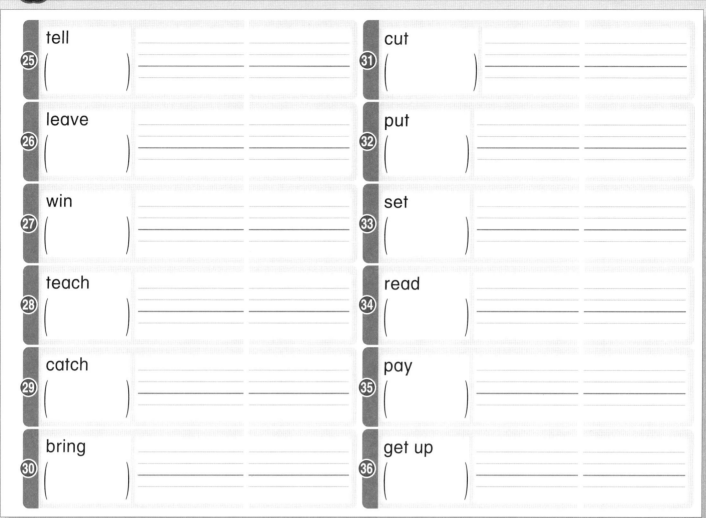

tell
㉕ (　　　　　　)

cut
㉛ (　　　　　　)

leave
㉖ (　　　　　　)

put
㉜ (　　　　　　)

win
㉗ (　　　　　　)

set
㉝ (　　　　　　)

teach
㉘ (　　　　　　)

read
㉞ (　　　　　　)

catch
㉙ (　　　　　　)

pay
㉟ (　　　　　　)

bring
㉚ (　　　　　　)

get up
㊱ (　　　　　　)

2 Search the textbook for these sentences in English and write them.

1 ぼくの木の実を食べた？

2 きみはランチを食べた？

3 あなたの部屋をそうじしましたか？

4 きみはお風呂に入った？

5 ぼくはお風呂に入ったよ。

6 彼は昨日学校に行きませんでした。

7 私は1ドル払いました。

8 私は朝7時前に家を出ました。

3 Complete the sentences using the past tense, and then translate the sentences into Japanese.

1 I _____ to school yesterday. (go)

( )

2 We _____ all the cake. (eat)

( )

3 It _____ hard last night. (rain)

( )

4 JJ _____ his leg last week. (break)

( )

5 Lisa and I _____ an interesting magic show. (watch)

( )

6 Kent _____ his hands before lunch. (wash)

( )

7 Sally _____ a pair of shoes two days ago. (buy)

( )

4 Rewrite the above sentences using not.

1 _____

2 _____

3 _____

4 _____

5 _____

6 _____

7 _____

5 Rewrite the sentences into **questions**. Answer them using both **yes** and **no**.

1
Q

A Yes, _____　No, _____

2
Q

A

3
Q

A

4
Q

A

5
Q

A

6
Q

A

7
Q

A

6 昨日したこと
What I did yesterday　Write about what you did yesterday.

1

2

3

4

1 WORDS Dictionary Write the phrases in Japanese, and then copy them in English.

① want to …
(   )

② enjoy …ing
(   )

③ stop …ing
(   )

④ practice …ing
(   )

⑤ keep …ing
(   )

⑥ go …ing
(   )

⑦ look forward to …ing
(   )

⑧ be good at …ing
(   )

⑨ how about …ing
(   )

⑩ thank you for …ing
(   )

⑪ start …ing
(   )

⑫ have a break
(   )

⑬ decide to
(   )

⑭ hope to
(   )

⑮ want to be
(   )

⑯ is prohibited
(   )

⑰ for our future
(   )

⑱ in the first row
(   )

2 Search the textbook for these sentences in English and write them.

1 ぼくは逆立ちをしたい。

2 Nelsonは魚つりが好きです。

3 Annは大きなホールで歌うのを楽しみにしています。

4 ゲームをして楽しみましょう。

5 ゲームするのをやめなさい。

6 手伝ってくれてありがとう。

7 私は一生懸命勉強しようと決めました。

8 英語を勉強することは私達の未来にとって大切なことです。

3 **Complete the sentences using the words and phrases below.**

① 私は買い物に行きたくありません。

I don't want ( ) shopping.

② ぼくは放課後にすることがない。

I have nothing ( ) after school.

③ 新しい場所に行くのは楽しいです。

( ) to new places in fun.

④ ぼくは今日、勉強をしたくない。

I don't want ( ) today.

⑤ 私の趣味はビンのふたを集めることです。

My hobby is ( ) bottle caps.

⑥ お婆さんは川に洗濯に行きました。

The old lady went to the river ( ) the clothes.

⑦ 私の母は朝早く散歩をするのが好きです。

My mother likes ( ) early in the morning.

⑧ 私の父は車を売る決心をしました。

My father decided ( ) his car.

⑨ ぼくは獣医になりたいです。

I want ( ) a vet.

⑩ 私たちは美しい夕日を見て楽しみました。

We enjoyed ( ) the beautiful sunset.

⑪ 私の父は英語を話すのが得意です。

My father is good at ( ) English.

⑫ Bill はここにもう一度来るのを楽しみにしています。

Bill is looking forward to ( ) here again.

⑬ 今食べる気にはなれません。

I don't feel like ( ) now.

to be	to do	to go	collecting	to sell	to study	to wash
to take a walk	watching	speaking	coming	going	eating	

4 Write the sentences, putting the words in order.

① あなたとお話しするのをとても楽しみました。 (really / you / with / enjoyed / I / talking) .

② 彼にまた会うのを楽しみにしています。 (looking / him / again / forward / seeing / to / I'm) .

③ 私の夢は外国に行くことです。 (dream / to / go / is / abroad / My) .

④ 毎日英語を話す練習をしなくてはなりません。 (every / day / I / have to / English / practice / speaking) .

5 Draw a line to connect the English and Japanese sentences.

① Let's get going. ● ● 来てくれてありがとう。

② Thanks for coming. ● ● もう行かなくちゃね。

③ It was nice meeting you. ● ● お会いできてよかった。

6 私の思い 1
My opinions 1 Complete the sentences with information about yourself.

1 It is interesting for me to

2 It is boring for me to

3 I need time to

4 I need some money to

5 I am looking forward to

6 I'm good at

1 WORDS Dictionary Write the words and phrases in Japanese, and then copy them in English.

① freeze (　　　　) ＿＿＿＿＿＿＿＿＿＿

② something (　　　　) ＿＿＿＿＿＿＿＿＿＿

③ earrings (　　　　) ＿＿＿＿＿＿＿＿＿＿

④ sneakers (　　　　) ＿＿＿＿＿＿＿＿＿＿

⑤ wig (　　　　) ＿＿＿＿＿＿＿＿＿＿

⑥ shaved ice (　　　　) ＿＿＿＿＿＿＿＿＿＿

⑦ Braille (　　　　) ＿＿＿＿＿＿＿＿＿＿

⑧ sheet music (　　　　) ＿＿＿＿＿＿＿＿＿＿

⑨ mittens (　　　　) ＿＿＿＿＿＿＿＿＿＿

⑩ socks (　　　　) ＿＿＿＿＿＿＿＿＿＿

⑪ someone (　　　　) ＿＿＿＿＿＿＿＿＿＿

⑫ bakery (　　　　) ＿＿＿＿＿＿＿＿＿＿

⑬ library (　　　　) ＿＿＿＿＿＿＿＿＿＿

⑭ police box (　　　　) ＿＿＿＿＿＿＿＿＿＿

⑮ head for (　　　　) ＿＿＿＿＿＿＿＿＿＿

⑯ be glad to (　　　　) ＿＿＿＿＿＿＿＿＿＿

⑰ be sorry to (　　　　) ＿＿＿＿＿＿＿＿＿＿

⑱ land on (　　　　) ＿＿＿＿＿＿＿＿＿＿

⑲ I want something. (　　　　) ＿＿＿＿＿＿＿＿＿＿

⑳ We go to school. (　　　　) ＿＿＿＿＿＿＿＿＿＿

㉑ It's time to go. (　　　　) ＿＿＿＿＿＿＿＿＿＿

2 Search the textbook for these sentences in English and write them.

1 ぼくはこごえています。

2 何か私に着るものをください。

3 それと何か温かい飲み物も。

4 私は今日するべき宿題がたくさんあります。

5 そこに行く道を聞くために交番に行きたい。

6 私はあなたに会えてうれしいです。

7 親切にも助けてくださってありがとう。

8 出発する時間です。
（行く時間です）

3 Look at the items from p. 72 in the textbook and write them in the correct categories.

1 something to wear

3 something to eat

2 something to drink

4 something to read

4 ～するための **Complete the sentences with appropriate English words and phrases.**

1 なにか読み物を持っていますか?

Do you have anything ＿＿＿＿＿＿＿＿＿＿ ?

2 だれか(ぼくを)手伝ってくれる人が必要です。

I need somebody ＿＿＿＿＿＿＿＿＿＿ me.

3 あなたに良いニュースがあるよ。何だと思う?

I have good news ＿＿＿＿＿＿＿＿＿＿ you.　Guess what.

4 それについてあなたに言うことは何もありません。

I have nothing ＿＿＿＿＿＿＿＿＿＿ to you about it.

5 そこに行く一番楽な方法はタクシーです。

The easiest way ＿＿＿＿＿＿＿＿＿＿ there is by taxi.

6 私に会う時間がありますか？

Do you have time ＿＿＿＿＿＿＿＿＿＿ me?

7 私のバッグを保管（キープ）する場所はありますか。

Do you have room ＿＿＿＿＿＿＿＿＿＿ my bag?

5 ～するために **Complete the sentences with appropriate English words and phrases.**

1 私たちは花見をしに公園に行きました。

We went to the park ＿＿＿＿＿＿＿＿＿＿ the cherry blossoms.

2 そのケーキを作るために卵が3つ必要です。

I need three eggs ＿＿＿＿＿＿＿＿＿＿ that cake.

3 私は３時に兄を迎えに空港へ行きます。

I'm going to the airport at 3 o'clock ＿＿＿＿＿＿＿＿＿＿ my brother.

4 御所に行くには4番バスに乗ってください。

Take bus No.4 ＿＿＿＿＿＿＿＿＿＿ to Gosho.

5 私たちは一緒に勉強するために図書館に行きました。

We went to the library ＿＿＿＿＿＿＿＿＿＿ together.

6 昨夜、大輔が私に会いに、ここに来ました。

Daisuke came here ＿＿＿＿＿＿＿＿＿＿ me last night.

7 ぼくたちは先生を驚かせるために机の後ろに隠れました。

We hid behind the desk ＿＿＿＿＿＿＿＿＿＿ our teacher.

6 ~して…/~するのに… **Complete the sentences with appropriate English words and phrases.**

1 （初めて会う人に）お会いできてうれしいです。

I am glad _____ you.

2 それを聞いて残念です。

I am sorry _____ it.

3 ご親切に助けてくれてありがとう。

It is kind of you _____ me.

4 それを見て驚きました。

I was surprised _____ that.

5 この水は飲んでも安全ですか?

Is this water safe _____ ?

6 これは答えるのに難しい質問です。

This is a difficult question _____ .

7 北海道は住むのにいい場所です。

Hokkaido is a nice place _____ .

私の思い2
7 **My Opinions 2** Complete the sentences with information about yourself.

1 I want to go to _____ to _____ .

2 I want to _____ .

3 It's great fun for me to _____ .

4 It is important to _____ .

5 It is easy for me to _____ .

to be rich	to study English	to make friends	to be famous
to play soccer	to help others	your own ideas	

英文とそれに関する質問文を聞いて、いちばん適切な答えを選びましょう。

No.1
① Last Saturday.　　② On a picnic.
③ Under a big tree.　④ Under a sunny tree.

🔘 1

No.2
① Every Saturday.　② Sometimes on Saturdays.
③ Every Sunday.　　④ Sometimes on Sundays.

🔘 2

No.3
① They climb Mt. Fuji.　② He climb Mt. Fuji.
③ They climbed Mt. Fuji.　④ He climbed Mt. Fuji.

🔘 3

No.4
① The fourth grade.　② The fifth grade.
③ The sixth grade.　　④ The seventh grade.

🔘 4

No.5
① To America.　　　　　② To Todai-ji.
③ Kenji didn't want to go.　④ John didn't want to go.

🔘 5

Listening Test ②

英文とそれに関する質問文を聞いて、いちばん適切な答えを選びましょう。

No.1
① A little better.　② Much better.
③ Fine.　　　　　④ Much worse.

🔘 6

No.2
① In the park.　　② On the phone.
③ At Tom's house.　④ At school.

🔘 7

No.3
① 7 o'clock.　② 11 o'clock.
③ 6 hours.　　④ 7 hours.

🔘 8

No.4
① To a florist.　② To her mother's house.
③ Home.　　　④ To a party.

🔘 9

No.5
①Left at the next corner, on the right.　② Right at the next corner, on the right.
③Left at the next corner, on the left.　④ Right at the next corner, on the left.

🔘 10

英語の会話を聞いて、それに関する質問に答えましょう。

No.1
① Yes, she did.   ② No, she didn't.
③ Yes, he did.   ④ No, he didn't.
CD 11

No. 2
① Iced coffee.   ② Iced tea.
③ Hot coffee.   ④ Milk tea.
CD 12

No. 3
① After school.   ② At school.
③ In three thirty.   ④ At three thirty.
CD 13

No. 4
① It will be fine.   ② It won't be raining.
③ It will be rainy.   ④ It will snow.
CD 14

No. 5
① By plane.   ② In plane.
③ By train.   ④ In train.
CD 15

英文とそれに関する質問文を聞いて、いちばん適切な答えを選びましょう。

No.1
① He walked.   ② He walks.
③ By car.   ④ He drove there.
CD 16

No. 2
① On Saturday.   ② Every day.
③ On Sunday.   ④ He wants to be a musician.
CD 17

No. 3
① She went swimming.   ② Last summer.
③ Sunny.   ④ Rainy.
CD 18

No. 4
① Science.   ② Math.
③ Reports.   ④ Her homework.
CD 19

No. 5
① Some apples.   ② Oranges.
③ Her aunt.   ④ Apple juice.
CD 20

英文とそれに関する質問文を聞いて、いちばん適切な答えを選びましょう。

No.1
① He doesn't know.
② No, he's too busy.
③ No, it's night.
④ Yes.
🔴 21

No.2
① Cindy is cold.
② Cindy's friend is cold.
③ Cindy has a cold.
④ Cindy's friend has a cold.
🔴 22

No.3
① Mr. Tanaka is in Japan.
② Mr. Tanaka is coming from Japan.
③ Mr. Tanaka is going back to Japan.
④ Mr. Tanaka wants a present.
🔴 23

No.4
① It's Emi's birthday.
② Emi has a present for her friend.
③ Emi doesn't have a present for her friend.
④ They are at Emi's house.
🔴 24

No.5
① Cathy is not there.
② Cathy doesn't live there.
③ Cathy has the wrong number.
④ Martin has the wrong number.
🔴 25

英語の会話を聞いて、それに関する質問に答えましょう。

No.1
① No, she went on Saturday.
② Yes, she did.
③ It was a good game.
④ No, she didn't.
🔴 26

No.2
① Yes, he does.
② Yes, he did.
③ No, he doesn't.
④ No, he didn't.
🔴 27

No.3
① Andy will.
② Andy's father will.
③ Mother will.
④ I will.
🔴 28

No.4
① They will eat it on Friday.
② At the pizza place.
③ No, they won't.
④ Yes, they will.
🔴 29

No.5
① No, she didn't.
② Yes, she did.
③ The window closed.
④ Lucy is cold.
🔴 30

英文とそれに関する質問文を聞いて、いちばん適切な答えを選びましょう。

No.1
① Tonight.
② This morning.
③ In this morning.
④ This evening.

31

No. 2
① For three months.
② In three months.
③ During three months.
④ Three months ago.

32

No. 3
① Because his teacher was late.
② Because he is always late.
③ Because he wasn't late.
④ Because the trains were late.

33

No. 4
① It was Chris's birthday.
② Chris was angry.
③ It was Jenny's birthday.
④ Jenny wasn't angry.

34

No. 5
① He bought sneakers.
② He found the monkey.
③ He took the money to the police.
④ He left it on the street.

35

Listening Test ⑧

英語の会話を聞いて、それに関する質問に答えましょう。

No.1
① He is looking for a red one.
② He doesn't have any money.
③ He is looking for a blue one.
④ No, he won't buy it.

36

No. 2
① No, she didn't.
② Yes, she did.
③ John was very kind to her.
④ John wasn't kind to her.

37

No. 3
① It opens at 9:15.
② It closes at 9:50.
③ It opens until 9:50.
④ It closes at 9:15.

38

No. 4
① To take a message.
② To ask what time the party starts.
③ To tell Cathy about the party.
④ To say hello.

39

No. 5
① She will go shopping.
② It will be fine.
③ She will sleep.
④ She will do her homework.

40

Let's try. 1

日本文の意味を表すように、① ～ ⑤ までならべかえましょう。

❶ 学校からの帰り道にケンに会いました。　I met (①Ken　②on　③home　④way　⑤my) from school.

I met _____ from school.

❷ これが私の町でいちばん高い建物です。　This is (①building　②tallest　③in　④the　⑤my) town.

This is _____ town.

❸ 放課後に野球をしてもいいですよ。　You (①play　②baseball　③after　④may　⑤school).

You _____

❹ 私は今日初めてマリ子に会いました。　I met (①for　②first　③Mariko　④the　⑤time) today.

I met _____ today.

❺ どれくらい京都に滞在するつもりですか？　How long (①you　②going　③stay　④are　⑤to) in Kyoto?

How long _____ in Kyoto?

❻ 私は、ユキをお誕生日パーティーに招待するつもりです。

I will (①Yuki　②to　③invite　④birthday　⑤my) party.

I will _____ party.

❼ 今年の夏休みは、何をするつもりですか？

What are (①you　②going　③do　④to　⑤during) this summer vacation?

What are _____ this summer vacation?

❽ 私は母よりずっと背が高いです。　I am (①taller　②much　③than　④mother　⑤my).

I am _____

❾ 遅れてすみませんでした。　I (①sorry　②late　③am　④I　⑤am).

I _____

❿ 私は何か冷たい飲みものがほしい。　I (①something　②drink　③to　④cold　⑤want).

I _____

⓫ 祖母はめがねをさがしています。　Grandmother (①for　②looking　③is　④her　⑤glasses).

Grandmother _____

Let's try. 2

（　）の中に最も適当なことばを選びましょう。

❶ Will you (＿＿＿＿＿) me the sugar, please?

　①some　②pass
　③do　④like

❷ You have to take (＿＿＿＿) your shoes when you enter the house.

　①on　②in
　③off　④of

❸ (＿＿＿＿＿) smoke. You are eighteen years old.

　①Isn't　②Not
　③Don't　④Aren't

❹ I like summer. (＿＿＿＿＿) about you?

　①How　②How many
　③Where　④Who

❺ Mt. Fuji is 3776 meters (＿＿＿＿＿).

　①long　②taller
　③high　④times

❻ My apartment is (＿＿＿＿＿) the second floor.

　①on　②in
　③at　④for

❼ Thank you very much (＿＿＿＿＿) the nice present.

　①in　②but
　③for　④did

❽ What (＿＿＿＿＿) you doing at nine o'clock last night?

　①are　②were
　③is　④am

❾ **A**: How much is this shirt?

　B: (＿＿＿＿＿＿＿＿＿＿＿)

　①870 yen.
　②45 minutes.
　③Thank you.
　④OK.

❿ **A**: Here's a present for you.　**B**: Thank you.

　A: (＿＿＿＿＿＿＿＿＿＿＿)

　①OK.
　②Of course.
　③You're welcome.
　④I am sorry.

⓫ **A**: Can you speak English?

　B: (＿＿＿＿＿＿＿＿＿＿＿)

　①I like it very much.
　②Just a little.
　③Thank you.
　④Yes, I do.

⓬ **A**: I feel much better today.

　B: (＿＿＿＿＿＿＿＿＿＿＿)

　①That's too bad.
　②Thank you.
　③I am sorry.
　④I am glad to hear that.

Let's try. 3

( )の中に最も適当なことばを選びましょう。

❶ A: Shall we go out to have dinner tonight?

B: (_____). I want to stay at home and watch TV.

①Yes, please.
②No, let's not.
③You're welcome.
④OK.

❷ A: Show me your photo. Who took it?

B: (_____)

①I like it.　　②My father did.
③That's my dog.　④This is a camera.

❸ A: (_____).

I could not understand what you said.

①Yes, please.　②I beg your pardon?
③Of course.　④I did.

❹ A: How about a cup of coffee?

B: (_____). I am not thirsty.

① Sugar, please.　② I like coffee.
③ I like tea.　④ No, thank you.

❺ A: (_____)

B:Yes, I am looking for a sweater for my mother.

①May I help you?　②Where is my mother?
③What is it?　④How much is it?

❻ A: This book is not mine. Whose book is this?

B: (_____)

①This is a book.　② It's hers.
③I like this book.　④No, thank you.

❼ A: What did Ken give you last night?

B: (_____)

① He gave you a nice bag.
② I gave him a nice bag.
③ He gave me a nice bag.
④ You gave me a nice bag.

❽ A: What month comes after June?

B: (_____)

①July does.　　②March does.
③August does.　④ July is.

❾ A: Shall I open the window?

B: (_____)

①Yes, let's.　　②Yes, please.
③You're welcome.　④That's all.

❿ A: What time did you eat lunch, today?

B: (_____)

①At lunch.　　②A hot dog.
③In the living room.　④At noon.

⓫ Why are you late (_____) school?

①on　②in　③for　④under

⓬ Be kind (_____) old people.

①for　②to　③on　④with

⓭ (_____) is the ninth month of the year.

①February　②November
③September　④October